WORKBOOK:

THE BILL OF OBLIGATIONS

A GUIDE TO THE HABITS OF GOOD CITIZENS

Thanks to my Reader.

TEN STEP GUIDE TO THE HABITS OF GOOD CITIZENS.

INSTRUCTIONS

1. HAVE A PEN/PENCIL WITH YOU AS YOU STUDY THIS WORKBOOK
2. IN THE "NOTES" SECTION, WRITE DOWN THE THOUGHTS THAT RAN THROUGH YOUR HEAD WHILE NAVIGATING EACH STEP
3. PRACTICE ALL YOU LEARN FROM THIS WORKBOOK.

NAME:

_____

_____

AGE:

_____

JOB:

_____

_____

_____

RELATIONSHIP STATUS:

_____

_____

This is an unendorsed workbook for Bill of Obligations by Richard Haass, which covers every core details of the book.

Political apathy is growing problem in the country and a lot of these things happen because of little or no awareness to your rights as a citizen, negligence or bad and poor leadership

From any angle you want to see it, this all concludes the said person as being a bad citizen to the country because he or she is not making use of their fundamental rights which also serves as a duty to the nation.

This workbook by Precious Works offers a practical

approach on how to become a better citizen.

This book is of great value and a must have for everyone who wants to grow good habits to becoming a better citizen!

<u>STEP 1</u>

"UNDERSTAND AND PLEDGE YOUR ANTHEM."

The very first identification of a great nation is seen in their anthem. It's simply the story of the nation being told.

You should be able to recite the anthem in your country as a good citizen and more than that, you should understand the story behind it and understand the anthem before you pledge to it.

Believe it or not, without love for your nation/ country, taking the initiative to understand your anthem won't be there. There would never be this push. Hence, the next cause of action is to develop that love for nation. Tin this love, buds respect for your nation, hence patriotism.

<u>WHAT TO DO?</u>

Look around you and study the goods things in your country. This is what buds the love for your nation. Also, take out time to learn and recite your anthem till it becomes a opart of you. Study and understand it.

<u>TIPS</u>

Not every country is the same. However, there is a lot of fascinating about yours as well. Find that and with it.

NOTES

_____

_____

_____

_____

_____

_____

_____

_____

_____

_____

_____

_____

_____

_____

_____

_____

_____

_____

STEP 2

"KNOW YOUR CONSTITUTION."

Every country has their unique constitution. It usually comprises of everything unique about the country. From the duties and obligations of delegated representatives to the country; the legislative arm, judiciary arm, and executive arm and even down to the duties and obligations of the citizens.

Also, it contains the enjoyable rights of the citizens like:

The right to live

The right to education

The right to personal life and property

It's only when you know your rights and duties that you can fully represent your country and defend it.

WHAT TO DO?

Get either the hard copy or soft copy of your constitution and learn it.

TIPS

Being intentional is very important.

<u>NOTES</u>

_____

_____

_____

_____

_____

_____

_____

_____

_____

_____

_____

_____

_____

_____

_____

_____

_____

_____

_____

STEP 3

"BE FAIR."

A lot of people can easily be influenced by things around them. These influences can be seen in favoritism and nepotism.

These things can be seen at work where you favor someone who is clearly unqualified for a job because you know this person over someone who actually merits that particular job. This is wrong.

Basically, as a good citizen, when you are in a position like being the CEO of a company, you should be fair enough to give out a job not on the grounds of bribery but on merit.

WHAT TO DO?

Be fair and modest in all you do.

TIPS

Even when working in the judiciary arm of government, impartiality is also required.

NOTES

STEP 4

"SHOW COMPASSION."

A little love and compassion goes a very long way. You don't need t be in the white house before you can reach out to help those around you. Start small.

You can show more love, care and compassion to those around you, your neighborhood.

All these things go a very long way. A little warmth and kindness can do a lot to help your neighborhood, community and your country at large.

<u>WHAT TO DO?</u>

Start volunteering.

<u>TIPS</u>

Compassion doesn't necessarily need to be financial. It can be as simple as lending a hand when necessary.

<u>NOTES</u>

STEP 5

"BE DISCIPLINED"

The problem with a lot of people is that they are easily swayed by public opinion or worse of all, bribed.

A lot of people has lost their moral compass band as such they can do any and everything because of money.

This only increases the country's problems because these people are not patriotic and therefore they cannot defend the country in time of need. That is why discipline is important.

As a good citizen, you need to be cultivating self-discipline so you'd be able turn down things that aren't just wrong for you but also the country at large.

<u>WHAT TO DO?</u>

Learn to live with contentment.

<u>TIPS</u>

In contentment, discipline becomes a lot easier.

NOTES

STEP 6

"HONESTY."

Honesty is the best policy am I right? Speaking the truth at all times is immensely important if you want to become a good citizen.

One of the best things you can do for your country is speaking the truth at all times. Also, there is this dignity that comes with it. You can't be bought basically.

Your truth is basically your untainted, raw and unique point of view.

This is one of the things you can do for country.

<u>WHAT TO DO?</u>

No matter how difficult it may seem, train your mind to always tell the truth at all times.

<u>TIPS</u>

Like a popular saying, the truth will set you free.

NOTES

STEP 7

"CLEAN AFTER YOURSELF."

In a developed country, there are garbage cans all over the city and loitering is avoided.

However, there are some people who would still choose to litter just because they want to.

Others would feel it unnecessary to throw out what needs to be thrown away and recycle what needs to be recycled.

All these things are what defines you as a bad citizen. You need to recycle when you need to, throw out your garbage, pick up after your dog when you go for a walk and basically clean up after yourself.

WHAT TO DO?

Develop the habit to clean your mess as soon as you make one.

TIPS

This doesn't just help you become a better citizen but also improves your health. As you get rid of the garbage, you also get rid of the germs too. As you get rid of the procrastination, you advance mentally as well.

<u>NOTES</u>

_____
_____
_____
_____
_____
_____
_____
_____
_____
_____
_____
_____
_____
_____
_____
_____
_____
_____
_____
_____

STEP 8

"DON'T STEAL."

A lot of people would say "it's not stealing when it's the government's funds. It's basically your money."

However, this is not true. Public funds remain public funds and if everyone uses it, then, there would be no money left to keep the country running.

So ensure you don't vandalize government property, steal from a hotel or basically anything that is not yours. Even from your neighborhood.

You are basically destroying your country and enslaving its citizens to poverty especially those that cannot afford much.

WHAT TO DO?

When you notice you can't abstain or stop stealing, try seeing a therapist.

TIPS

What's the point of stealing when what you steal wouldn't last long?

NOTES

STEP 9

"RESPECT THE LAW."

Laws are made for a reason and trust me, they are not made to be broken.

These laws are meant to be abode and not just by low country folk but by everyone.

A lawless country suffers:

- Corruption
- Bribery
- Terrorism

All these injustice are as a result of a lawless or breaking of these laws and if you're being honest, these things and a lot more is the problem with the country today.

WHAT TO DO?

Become a respectable law-abiding citizen.

TIPS

These are the little ways you can help your country on your end.

NOTES

STEP 10

"VOTE."

Like I earlier said, a lot of people are politically apathetic. They don't care about the affairs of their country and this is a very dark label of bad citizenship.

Voting is not just a way of expressing your opinion or doing what you feel is best for your country but it is also a way to show that you support the franchise system and are making good use of your rights.

A lot of people complain about the faults in their countries but when it's time to speak up and take a stand they relent which is the same thing as saying and doing nothing.

WHAT TO DO?

Take a step and vote in the next elections.

TIPS

The government is the people so you have every right to vote.

NOTES

THE END OF THIS WORKBOOK.

AFTER FOLLOWING THE ABOVE-STATED STEPS, EVALUATE YOURSELF AND REPEAT THE SAME STEPS!

HOW HAS THIS WORKBOOK HELPED YOU?

_____

_____

_____

_____

_____

_____

_____

_____

_____

_____

_____

_____

_____

_____

_____

_____

PRIVATE NOTES

EXTRAS